Uncertain Seasons

poems by

Ruth Harper

Finishing Line Press
Georgetown, Kentucky

Uncertain Seasons

Copyright © 2023 by Ruth Harper
ISBN 979-8-88838-083-3 First Edition
All rights reserved under International and Pan-American Copyright Conventions. No part of this book may be reproduced in any manner whatsoever without written permission from the publisher, except in the case of brief quotations embodied in critical articles and reviews.

Acknowledgments

Grateful acknowledgements to the following journals and books where some of the poems in this chapbook have been published or will soon appear:

Pasque Petals: "At the Nature Park;" "Picnic;" "Late Summer, Open Field" (third place winner, landscape category, South Dakota Poetry Society competition); "Wingsprings" (second place winner, landscape category, South Dakota Poetry Society competition)
Dakota Heritage: "Fall Arrives" (as "First Morning")
Peril & Promise: Essays on Community in South Dakota and Beyond: "Her Words"
South Dakota Magazine: "South Dakota"
South Dakota in Poems: "Syllables of Snow" (as "February Snow")

Publisher: Leah Huete de Maines
Editor: Christen Kincaid
Cover Art: *Uncertain Seasons* is by Meghan Peterson
Author Photo: MaryJo Benton Lee
Cover Design: Elizabeth Maines McCleavy

Order online: www.finishinglinepress.com
also available on amazon.com

Author inquiries and mail orders:
Finishing Line Press
PO Box 1626
Georgetown, Kentucky 40324
USA

Table of Contents

Winter
- South Dakota 1
- Syllables of Snow 2
- December's Encompassing Silence 3
- Decades of Zhivago 4
- Necklace for My Mother 6
- Longest Night, Brightest Planets 7
- January Thaw 9

Spring
- Rebirth 10
- Songs of Spring 11
- Sky-blue Quilt 12
- Coming Rain 13
- Pandemic Baby 14
- On Turning 70 16

Summer
- Wingsprings 18
- Late Summer, Open Field 19
- Picnic 20
- Liminal Moment 22
- At the Nature Park 23
- Her Words 24

Autumn
- Fall Arrives 25
- Yesterday and Today 26
- The Book of Ruth 27
- Hymn after Hymn 28
- Dakota Moon 29
- Window Boxes 30
- Northern Ash 31

With Thanks 32
Discussion Questions 33

Winter

South Dakota

An aboriginal state,
its maps are mistranslations of winter counts,
its towns camps of the uninvited.
Songs and ceremonies
of high plains, Black Hills, prairies
hold light
and a search for redemption.

Made of stars and sand,
this land longs for spirits
that will not come now.
The spirits have nowhere
to return to;
they are exiled, and exist
only as secrets
or in stories
told to grandchildren.

Then it happens
among the holy ones.
Transformed by language—
by hope, by prayer—
we gather energy
that holds us together
and commit to honor promises
that were never meant
to be kept.

Winter

Syllables of Snow

Inuits have 400 words for snow.
In South Dakota
snow possesses its own intricate vocabulary
uttered in ancient choruses
beyond what the human ear
detects.
Blizzards chant in triumphant
tones of Tibetan throat-singing monks;
their incantations
soar across empty prairies,
summoning spirits
of endless winter.

A simple snowfall
is quiet, hushed, silent.
Only ears of wakeful owls
and restless infants
may discern its
midnight murmurs
exhaled in fresh and
startling spills
of silver shining in moonlight.

At sunrise,
snow speaks
in simple, civil sentences
about February,
survival,
cleanliness,
cold.

December's Encompassing Silence

High in a sterile sky
the moon's bony grin
broadens each night.

White lights in houses
set at angles etched into frozen prairie
glimmer like rows of luminaries.

Low on the horizon
they gleam against darkness and
December's encompassing silence.

Venus is a pearl
I can almost touch
through backyard branches.

Winter

Decades of Zhivago

This story is written by birches on snow,
punctuated by endless train tracks through icy forests.

I read *Doctor Zhivago* at age 16.
My English teacher stood over me and scolded:
You are not old enough to appreciate this book,
but I loved it.
I identified with Tonia, the wife,
and thought Yuri's betrayal unforgivable
despite the circumstances.

I read it again at 35,
having experienced life's duplicities,
my own opaque justifications, reconstructed hopes.
It was too late to tell Miss Struthers
that she was right; it was as if
I'd encountered entirely different characters.
I identified with no one, no longer being
as trusting as Tonia, never as irresistible as Lara,
rarely as desperate as Yuri.

And now, age 70, I read *Doctor Zhivago* for the third time.
Today, the only voice in my ear is Yuri's,
idealism worn as thin as his wedding band.
Like him, my devotion to contemplation and art
is revealed by actions more menial than grand,
through attention to leaves, stones, birds—
ideas for poems on scraps of paper
stuffed like receipts into pockets.
What once seemed distant and exotic
is now timeless, personal.

No question, the joy of connection
is often paid for in risk, pain, regret—
yet I have learned, like Yuri, that love
is why we exist.

Though my reading of the book changes over time,
Zhivago prevails
in the eternal search for human intimacy, despite the cost;
the bitter price of deception, its blades cutting in all directions;
and the vast Russian landscape,
where this story is written again and again
by birches against fields of snow.

Winter

Necklace for My Mother

The leafless aspen
dangles droplets
glistening
in perfect intervals

like the pearls
I brought Mother from India,
the ones I will soon wear
to her memorial service.

I take a deep breath
and nod
to the prisms in the tree
that cede my sorrow to the sky.

Longest Night, Brightest Planets

On winter's solstice
humans in northern latitudes
turn again to the light.
This year, the Christmas star,
in reality two planets
distant from us and each other
seem, from Earth's plane,
to converge above the prairie's horizon.
Jupiter's majesty pairs
with the elegance of Saturn
and her eternally orbiting mystical rings.

A star? A portent? An omen?
What do we make of it
as we drive home
hushed and humbled?
The ancients
created mythologies that
meander down millennia
of campfires and star gazing.

Did magi follow a stellar sign
to Bethlehem, to a baby? Unlikely.
Shall we, like William the Conqueror
upon seeing Halley's Comet,
assign personal significance
to the magnificent gesture of atoms
dancing in space?

Winter

On this longest night
of the loneliest year,
two planets align
beneath a gleaming crescent moon,
reminding us
during bleak pandemic days
that always
in this astonishing,
indifferent universe
extraordinary beauty awaits
within the depths of darkness.

January Thaw

It arrives as my mother always predicted—
sun re-angling its route across the roof of sky.
Bare trees cast hieroglyphic shadows;
puddles float ice chunks fat as dumplings.
The streets are streams of melting snow.

It's still cold,
but there's a soft staccato,
the pleasing percussion
of water dripping from every surface—
and, in the distance,
birdsong.

Spring

Rebirth

> *It's just beyond yourself, it's where you need to be.*
> —David Whyte

Wind off the frozen lake is arctic.
Distant stretches of open water
flash deep blue among
ice chunks bobbing and glowing,
a million spilled crystals,
sharp edges spinning sunlight.
My own jaggedness is invisible.
I walk the lakeside path on this Good Friday,
exhaling stress with each breath.
A bald eagle soars, circles, settles—
silhouetted in a distant oak.

By Saturday morning, gusts have swept
all shards to the shoreline.
Gone is the heron poised yesterday in the shallows;
the pair of Canada geese seeks inland shelter.
I sit in the sun, wanting to reflect, be grateful—
my cheeks wet with tears.

At dawn on Easter Sunday
birdsong I don't recognize
draws me to the window:
two pileated woodpeckers yip like coyotes
and hammer in circles around an old maple.
The resurrection, the only one certain to me,
is right here, right now—and it is enough.

Spring

Songs of Spring

Latticework of emerging leaves,
translucent greens and yellows,
slanting sunward
into sapphire skies.

The willow dangles arched arms,
flaxen as forsythia,
while lindens litter boulevards
with dirty brown leaf casings,
revealing tiny tender-green tongues
weighting each laden branch.

Red-twig dogwoods repaint their scarlet skeletons;
frost-burned yews rebirth
in emerald pointillism;
lilacs grip tight fists of scent.
Still-bare locust trees
are comforted by serried choirs
of song sparrows.
The crimson cardinal croons
his throaty love song
from the top of the Black Hills spruce.

Mid-June these high plains fade
to summer's perennial gold and brown;
but today,
this bright May morning,
each newborn leaflet is a verdant prayer flag
singing an exultant yes
to spring.

Spring

Sky-blue Quilt

Bursting at seams
etched by jet planes—
Rapid City to Chicago,
Fargo to Kansas City,
Winnipeg to Omaha—
cirrus strands escape, tease apart
randomly stitched borders.
Thin mists crochet a shawl
draping earth's bare western shoulder
as yet another contrail staples the sky—
Denver to Minneapolis.
The April breeze
inhales deeply, laughs aloud,
easily unhems another corner of heaven.

SPRING

Coming Rain

The sky draws bold
slanting pencil lines
shading the southern horizon.

This day, a murky charcoal drawing
of sullen clouds
sketches steel-gray mountains
rising above a distant plain.

Unmistakable,
the scent of spring:
wet / fresh / alive / organic—
it arrives like earth's exhalation.

All is erased
in the sudden downpour.

Spring

Pandemic Baby
(for Miles Richard)

Six days before the world closed,
you join us:
perfect and oblivious,
wanting only mama's milk
and everyone's love,
plentiful even in this strange time.

Though the pregnancy
in which you grew
from single cell
to tadpole
to frog
to infant boy
was stressful,
and your birth terrifying,
you squint through swollen eyes,
exuding calm wisdom
we come to know as
your sweet temperament.

Your tiny body heals us,
makes us whole, hopeful;
your needs demand responses
we compete to comfort.
Your elusive smiles bestow absolution
on lockdown days when we do nothing
but watch for the light
to ignite in your shining blue eyes.

Spring

In these silent moments,
we hold you and love you
as if nothing is wrong,
there is no virus among us,
no fear,
only the small planet of your flawless self,
a reality scented with the magic of the newly born.
And we, your grandparents, orbit
like ancient sages
seeking only the warmth and radiance
emanating from you.

Spring

On Turning 70

> *Do not grow old, no matter how long you live. Never cease to stand like curious children before the great mystery into which we were born.*
> —Albert Einstein

As each day begins,
I read a Psalm and a poem,
pause to breathe, to be grateful.
The Psalmist writes, "create in me a clean heart,"
but says nothing of the ache in my hip.
Still, I head out for a walk.

Dakota-blue sky is visible through trees
that spread fingertips tinged with green.
Corrugated clouds scud along
on a breeze that smells of fresh mud,
dead leaves, hidden blossoms.
Robins are everywhere, chirping, chasing, circling.
I round a corner and startle two Canada geese into their pond.

Always, always something new:
a word to look up, a poem to ponder,
a recipe, a book, a writing prompt.
There is the delight of new friends,
even at this age,
and the comfort of those I have loved for years.

Spring

My grandsons show me every day
how to see the world with joy.
The one-year-old says, *wow-wow-wow!*
even to an empty street—
and I stand with him, wide-eyed and smiling—
just another curious child
before the great, eternal mystery.

Summer

Wingsprings
    For Craig Howe and Charles Woodard

Perched in an ancestral landscape,
pages of rolling hills unfurl into forever,
punctuated only
by the butte marking home,

we pause to say good morning:
hi hanni wasté.

The enormous innocent sky
holds meadowlark mornings
in its open palm; later,
evening's embers spill
from its loosening grasp
into chasms of darkness.

Tall-grass prairie murmuring
with dull wood ticks and bejeweled dragonflies
knows coyote songs,
curious cattle,
and more than a few
intrepid humans.

Each person
brings a rock to the cairn at the gate;
each stone
a story
and a promise.

I will see you again later:
toksa ake wacinyankinkte ye.

Summer

Late Summer, Open Field

Kneeling in the meadow
I observe the beetle's boudoir,
rich golden grasses
damp with tears of dew,
a garden of silk
beneath my booted foot.

The scarlet robin
strides with bravery
or indifference toward
my silent presence.

Nearby bees inhale
the many-breasted roses'
dense well of fruity musk,
a year of scent
in each narrow heart.

High in cottonwoods
birds with dark beaks crouch
over streaked eggs,
the solitary woodpecker
a maestro
of potent nods.

I move among dynasties
in the open green field,
tasting death in the
disconsolate rain
as winter looms,
a distant shadow
in its dark frock coat.

Note: This is a response to a writing prompt to use as many words as possible from Sylvia Plath's poem "The Beekeeper's Daughter" in an original poem.

Summer

Picnic

At this picnic
I can do anything.
Of course, the usual will occur—
eating, drinking, wandering quietly
into the woods for illicit kisses.
I am likely to read a book under a tree,
hold a sleeping infant,
admire the osprey's fierce silhouette
above the dead cottonwood
near the water.

I may wonder why a cloud floats
from my picnic basket as I open it,
whether the sudden breeze will follow me
all the way home,
if that astonishing kiss means nothing
or everything.

At this picnic,
if I pay attention (still and silent)
I will see my mother
in the butterfly
that lingers on my shoe.

I will hear finches sing
and follow their melodies
deep into the forest,
knowing I am safe
as their flashing yellow or red
are signs along my path.

Summer

How does this picnic end?
If I am patient, I will see
my mother again
in the thin light of dawn
crouched with her old metal coffee pot
over the campfire,
waiting for me, smiling.

Summer

Liminal Moment

Lying on the dock at night
I am a child again;
weathered wooden boards sway like a cradle
gently kept in motion
by a watchful mother's foot,
her hands busy elsewhere.

A sky full of summer stars dances,
reflected in the water's flickering surface.
Day noises fade to random chirps
of settling birds and the baritone of tree frogs.

Lying on the dock at night,
I feel ageless, suspended
in space between water and stars.
My breathing slows
to the cadence of the universe.
I am held in the mystery of this moment,
surrounded by what oddly feels like love.

SUMMER

At the Nature Park

An opaque slice of half moon
grins into the silver mirror of the prairie pond
this clear August morning.
I stroll around still water,
moving from dancing shadows
among sighing cottonwoods
to full sunlit silence along the bold line of shore.
Fall's first singular red leaf waves
its gaudy little flag
above majestic stands of goldenrod,
snowdrifts of bursting milkweed pods.
Butterflies red/gold/black
blink wings open/shut/open around my head,
murmuring of migrations.
I have nowhere to be but here.

Summer

Her Words

For Linda Hasselstrom after a poetry reading at Augustana University (Sioux Falls)

Her keen eyes
snap and shine, head tilted
like the birds she observes closely
on sprawling plains
and in clapboard Cheyenne.
She is mindfully awake,
attentive to the pacific grace of grasslands;
alert to their understated dramas—
> kettles of hawks,
> exaltations of larks,
> medleys of wildflowers;

her vigilance constant
as a hovering kestrel
alive with vivid, heedful language
as the rest of us drink lattes
and neglect to look up.

Her hands that know how to work cattle also
dance elegantly with words,
> rise with the black-crowned night heron,
> hail curious neighbors.

Her well-worn boots stride abandoned cemeteries.
She is the solitary mourner
at eroded gravestones,
a stranger's infant daughters,
prairie lambs long forgotten.
The poet ponders whether her parents,
resting elsewhere in this clay,
understand at last
that words are her beloved children.

Autumn

Fall Arrives

Just before dawn
a thunderstorm
shoulders its way through town
like a lumberjack on the way
to a big breakfast.
Behind the rain
north winds rush
unimpeded down the high plains,
a door in Manitoba kicked open.

The sky opens its arms
to a vast and shining cold front.
A half-moon floats low,
silent and
translucent as a tear
in the water-colored west.

On this first fall morning,
red leaves line the trail.
Wild sunflowers dance on the breeze,
as geese noisily round up their cousins
for the long pilgrimage south.

Autumn

Yesterday and Today

Just yesterday the front-yard aspen
wildly jangled
plump arms of golden bangles;
today
it grips tattered parchment notes
with skeletal fingers.

Out back
the moody evergreen shrugs,
empties pockets of sparrows,
bright copper pennies
on dark sod.

Autumn

The Book of Ruth

I loved my husbands,
both of them.
But I was devoted to my mother-in-law
and refused to leave her.
People wondered why
I remained in Israel
away from my family and faith.
But I had learned much
of compassion
from my Jewish husband
and his kind mother.
Nothing in Moab
called to me
anymore.
Caring for Naomi
gave me reason to
rise in the morning
to see her smile,
to gather grain to feed us.
Tales of my loyalty
became fabled.
My story is even in the Bible,
where few women matter.
I never expected to be remembered
beyond my own small circle,
especially for giving comfort
to an older woman.
But here I am
in the pages of history:
widow, immigrant, convert.
Nothing legendary.
Just a woman who said to another
I promise
you will not die alone.

Autumn

Hymn after Hymn

My grandmother was always old:
permed white curls, saggy house dresses, sturdy shoes.
Sometimes, when she visited us,
I walked in on her praying at the side of the bed—
kneeling with hands clenched, eyes closed—
for what seemed like a very long time.
Her world was small and sober;
how did she have so much to say to God?
At night, she played the piano, hymn after hymn,
singing in a tremulant soprano, a lonely sparrow.

My father was always young,
at least younger than my friends' parents.
He too was a musician: singer, pianist, organist.
Fourth of her five sons, he was my grandmother's joy
because he became a pastor; he wore suits. After
my mother's death, he came to live in my small prairie town.
His first request was a piano, and I got him one.
His sight had failed, but he knew hundreds of pieces by heart;
many evenings at his assisted living home
he played that piano, hymn after hymn.

I have always felt the same age,
a Boomer in jeans and cotton shirts.
I abandoned piano, then guitar,
convinced I lacked talent.
Now, a grandmother myself, with dimming vision,
I wander to the piano at the end of the day.
I am beginning to understand the solace
of chords reaching resolution when so much else
is chaos. Hymn after hymn, I play—
realizing in wonder that I am good enough.

Autumn

Dakota Moon
> *At the dedication of South Dakota State University's first
> American Indian Education & Culture Center, November, 2010;
> for April Eastman*

Melon-orange crescent moon
floats
in darkening west as
Dakota prayers
re-sanctify this space.

Everyone, everything here
knows
these words belong with this land;
the cottonwoods stand straight and silent,
bare branches raised like
a congregation of witnesses.

Long before
Europeans platted prairies
with treaties/fences/deeds of sale,
true clear rivers ran to green valleys;
ancient plains unfolded into infinity;
and songs like these
were sung
in this sacred place
beneath the all-seeing moon.

Autumn

Window Boxes

Geraniums and snapdragons,
reluctant to bloom this summer,
decide mid-October
to put on a scandalous display:
deep scarlet, magenta, plum,
propped up by
desiccated sticks and stems,
weathered leaves mottled
like an old woman's hands.

The flowers cry out:
> *look at me,*
> *notice me,*
> *I am still here!*

I think of mother
starting hospice this month,
flirting with the new night nurse.

Autumn

Northern Ash

One October morning—
silent, sun-filled—
the leaves
shrug, sigh,
and let go.

It happens:

> *fall*
> *gently*
> *now.*

Yellow mittens twirl
two, three, twenty times,
drift
into a soft pile
at the base of each tree.

Within moments, it seems,
naked branches
stretch bare fingers
into a shining sky.

With Thanks

Original cover artwork, "Uncertain Seasons," is by Meghan Peterson. Find her remarkable work here: meg.mariah27@gmail.com or @megmariah27 on Instagram.

Deepest thanks to Charles Woodard and Annette Langlois Grunseth, who provided generous, insightful editing and feedback on this manuscript. Anything that "works" in this collection does so because you advised, "find another word" or "would it kill you to add a figure of speech?" Thank you.

Many offered inspiration and/or encouragement, most notably Larry Rogers; others to whom I am especially grateful include Christine Stewart-Nuñez, Jane Fried, Jessica Lankford, MaryJo Lee, Mary Alice Haug, Phyllis Cole-Dai, Ruby Wilson, and additional kind friends, including my wonderful book group: Della Tschetter, Marla Muxen, Jeannie Manzer, and Nan Steinley.

Personal, heartfelt gratitude and love to Elizabeth Harper Bailey (Libby) and Margaret Elise Miller (Maggie), my finest creations, and to my mother, Shirley Spencer Harper (1930-2011), who substituted Robert Frost for the Bible story after breakfast whenever my father left us alone.

Discussion Questions

Note: these can also be used as writing prompts.

1. Birds are mentioned in many of these poems. In South Dakota (and elsewhere, of course), birds migrate with the seasons. Their arrivals and departures mark our lives as surely as a calendar. Which birds do you notice and what do they mean to you?

2. In "Hymn after Hymn" I write about something I saw (and heard) my grandmother do, then saw (and heard) my father do, an activity—playing piano—that I now find myself doing regularly after a hiatus of many years. What do you see in yourself today of a grandparent or parent that surprises you? How do these qualities or behaviors link you to the past, to your family, to a world you knew as you were growing up?

3. I wrote "On Turning 70" with joy. What do you love about being the age you are?

4. Three of the poems in this collection ("South Dakota," "Wingsprings," and "Dakota Moon") reference the people who were in South Dakota long before European settlers arrived. Many Native people live here still. Who first lived where you now reside? What do you know of their culture(s)? What have you learned from the people indigenous to the area?

5. At least two of the poems in this collection are about being drawn deeply into a moment in nature ("At the Nature Park" and "Liminal Moment"). Describe a time outdoors that captured your spirit so intensely that you wanted to remember it always.

6. "Decades of Zhivago" is about reading the same book at three points in life and having distinctly different reactions to it. Have you had this experience? Which book(s) have you reread and found meaningful (or not!) in new ways? How have you changed over time, do you think? What underlies new reactions to a familiar book?

7. Three poems reference my mother at the end of her life. "Window Boxes" is about her approaching death; "Necklace for My Mother" describes a morning just after her death; "Picnic" contains several surreal images, including that of my mother smiling at me over a campfire a year after she died. Each of us remembers enduring the death of someone we love, of perhaps focusing in grief on something like a sturdy tree, or raindrops, or dying flowers. What comes to mind as you reflect on a difficult loss? What in nature has sustained you or helped you feel connected to a larger, ongoing world?

8. One thing I often struggle with as I write poetry is the difference between a vivid memory or image and an effective poem. What is powerful in the moment (as an experience) is often not powerful on the page (as a poem). What would it take to turn a memory of yours into a poem? Would you like to try?

RUTH HARPER is Professor Emerita of Counseling and Human Development at South Dakota State University, where she coordinated the college counseling and student affairs administration specialties for over 20 years. She co-authored four books in her field and has special interest in American Indian college student success, the role of tribal colleges in South Dakota, and college student mental health. Ruth holds a B.A. from Cornell College (Mt. Vernon, IA), an M.Ed. from the University of Wisconsin-Oshkosh (Oshkosh, WI), and a Ph.D. from Kansas State University (Manhattan, KS).

Ruth lives in Brookings, South Dakota, and is married to Lawrence Rogers, mother to adult daughters Libby and Maggie, and Nana to grandsons Max and Miles. She is currently on the board of the local PFLAG (Parents, Families, & Friends of Lesbians & Gays+) and the Advisory Council of the Boys & Girls Club of the Northern Plains (Brookings).

For Ruth, reading fiction and poetry has been a lifelong joy; in retirement, writing poetry is a meaningful pursuit and challenge.

www.ingramcontent.com/pod-product-compliance
Lightning Source LLC
Chambersburg PA
CBHW022125090426
42743CB00008B/1010